The Tents of the Tribe

Ibrahim al-Awaji

The Tents of the Tribe

A Bilingual Collection of Arabic Poetry

Translated from the Arabic by
Maryam Ishaq Al-Khalifa Sharief

Echoes

British Library Cataloguing-in-Publication Data
A catalogue record for this book is available from
the British Library

ISBN 1 873395 60 4 Hb
ISBN 1 873395 61 2 Pbk

This edition first published 1996 by
Echoes
26 Westbourne Grove
London W2 5RH

Typeset by Group E, London

Contents

The Tents of the Tribe   9

The Migration of the Moon   21

Palermo   31

When Stones Foliate   41

The Source   47

Soliloquy in a Boat   55

The Remains of the Years   67

Exile   75

Princess of Eyes   85

Challenge   91

Rainbow   97

O My Bird   101

In the Grotto   107

A Sentiment   111

A Fairy and a Jar   115

Two Travellers   119

Contents

Embrace	123
Love's Playful Child	129
Capri	133
Free Love for All	141
Love May Not Be Bought	157
O Trees of the Acacia	165
Dollar	169

The Poems

خيام القبيلَة

١

و كنت أظن بأن غــرامي

بصحرا تنام

على خاصريها جميع النجوم

وتغفو

وتبعثُ في التائهينَ

الأمل

ويعرف أسرارها الأنبياء

والصالحون

The Tents of the Tribe

I

I once believed,

That my beloved dwelt

In the desert.

Upon whose flanks,

All the stars drowsed and slumbered.

A desert,

Which awakened the

Hope of wanderers.

And, whose secrets are known

To the Prophets

And to the saintly.

ويفرشها الأقحوان

بفصل الربيع

بلون الخيّال

ويرسم عذب النسيم

على وجنتيها

صنوفَ القبل

حكاية أمسي

المخضب بريح الخزامى

وعشق الشقاء

وحسي بأني

بقايا الأزل

A desert,

Which in Springtime is covered

In camomile flowers

The colour of dreams.

And, where the sweetness

Of breath draws on its cheeks

All kinds of kisses.

A desert,

Where the story of my past

Is drenched in fragrance of the

khozamah[1] flower.

And, where my passion

For the taste of affliction and

My very sense of being

Are felt like remnants

Of eternity.

---

1. Also called khozam. A wild plant of the desert with a sweet odour and a flower which resembles the violet.

٢

دخلت مراراً
خيام القبيلةْ
وراقصت كل الحسان
وبارزت فرسَانها
وخلت
بأن الحسان سواء
لأنك ما كنت
في الخَدر سَاعة كنت
تطلين خلفَ
ثقوب الرواق
ويوم تعبت
وصرت بحال
شـــــلل

٣

وهاجرت في اليم
أبحث في التيه

II

I, frequently entered

The tents of the tribe;

To dance with the beautiful women.

To make battle with the Knights.

I, believed all beauties

To be one and the same.

For you were not there

In the tent with me,

On that day when,

Strained by exhaustion

I fell paralysed.

III

I, voyaged in the sea

Searching in the wilderness

عن طرف التيه

وما كنت في زورق

وما كنت أعرفُ

فن السباحة

ولا المَوْج

وكنت أشوقك

كنت أتوقك

وفيك ثمل

وصرت أفتش

عن ناظريك

وأسأل كل المحار

وكل شعاب البحار

For its very edge.

I, was not in a boat
And I knew not
How to swim,
Nor about the way
Of the waves.

I, pined for you
And longed to find you
Drunk in the abandon
Of a languorous mood.

I, began to search
For your eyes.
I asked every shell
And every reef
In the sea

وكادت قواي تخور

وجاء نداء الصحارى

العتيق

يذكرني

بأن نبات الصحارى مثلي

يعرف كيف يقاوم

صوت الملل

٤

فكان صمودي

نجَاتي

لأنك جئت

تقودين حص البحار

وكل اللآلي

وبين يديك

وعاء هواء

Until my strength
Was almost drained.

Suddenly, the ancient call
From the desert came to me
Reminding me, that desert
Flora such as myself
Know how to resist
The voice of ennui.

IV

Thus, in my firm stance
I found salvation.
For you came to me
Escorting all the gems
And pearls from the sea.

In your hands you held
A vessel of air,

وجرعة ماء

وقلت بأن البحار

كصحرائنا

غموض وحبّ

وأنت تحب

فصرت بقربك

مثل سماك البحار

أعوم

كما كنت

بالأمس

فوق شداد الجمل.

A drink of water.

And you said that

The seas, like our desert

Are made of mystery

And of love.

And you are in love.

When I am near you,

I am like a fish

In the sea.

I, can swim now

Like I used to

In days of old

On the saddle of a camel.

هجرة قمَر

أهجرت بلادك يا قمر

وسهولاً كنت أناجيها

وحقولاً في ضوئك حالمة

وصحارى كنت تسليها

وقوافل تختال على مهل

تستهوي التيه ويهويها

The Migration of the Moon

In truth—O Moon

Have you forsaken your own homeland?

Land of soft plains with which

I once communed

And of fields turning dreamy

Beneath your light.

Land of deserts which, in bygone days

You often consoled

And of caravans moving slowly

In vast expanses of catching lure.

اتركت السمار بلا سمر

ورعاة العيس وحاديها

وزفاف القرية ملحمة

للحب وصفو أهاليها

من ذا يحييه اذا غربت

شمس وتعتم واديها

ماذا أسرى بك يا قمر

عن أرض كنت تواسيها

In truth—O Moon

Have you left the company which gathered at night

With no tale to tell ?

Those herders of camels of choicest breed

Who chanted a song as

Onward, they prompted a drove.

What—O Moon

Of guests at a village wedding

That epic tribute

Paid to love?

Who—but you

Shall enliven the nights

As the sun goes down

And the valley is darkened?

What—O Moon

أثلوج الألب وقمتها

أغرتك فرمت أعاليهَا

ورحلت بصفوك دون أسى

أترى أسلتك غوانيهَا

ونسيت العشاق بقريتنا

وبنجاوى كنت تناغيهَا

Compelled you to rove in the night

Far from a land

You once consoled?

Have the snows in the Alps

And their peaks

Enticed you to seek

Their far off heights?

So, you departed

With a limpid countenance

Free of sorrow.

Have the enchantresses

Made you forget?

Have they made you forsake

The lovers of our village

Whose intimate address

You tenderly returned?

وتركت مراتع كنت بها

رمز الأسفار وهاديهَا

الأنك تخجل يا قمر

من حال حل بواديهَا

ومن الاحباط يلاحقهَا

ويعشعش فوق روابيها

أم أنك تأنف يا قمر

ان تفضح عمق مآسيها

Or the once joyous pastures
Where still you remain
A guide to the traveller,
A sign to the wanderer.

Can it be—O Moon
That you recoil with shame
From the sight of misfortune
Which now befalls
The surrounding country?

From thwarted hopes
Which haunt the land
And fester everywhere
Atop the hills.

Or is it—O Moon
That you spurn to expose
The depth of misery?

وتعرّي زيف مظاهرها

وتبين فرقة أهليهَا

أم انك ترفض يا قمر

ان تصبح ضم مواشيها

ويصير ضياؤك مركبة

يلهو السمّار بناديها

28

Or lay open that guile of appearance

Revealing a people in strife?

Or is it—O Moon

That you shun becoming

Another one of the cattle?

Another one of the crowd?

Or that your light

Should be reduced to a mere carrying vessel

For the boon companions

Whose time is idled wantonly at play?

بالرمو

١

بالرمو
يا ابنة العشاق
والتيّاه
والقرصان
يا طفلة شاخت
وما زالت صبيّة
وبحاجبيها
يختبي الاجهاد
والتاريخ

Palermo

I

Palermo.

O daughter of lovers,

Of wanderers

And of pirates.

O little girl

Who turned aged,

Yet a young maiden

She still remains.

On her eyebrows

History hides

Together with exhaustion.

وتفوح من أنفاسها

عبرا طريّةٌ

رافقت صاحبتي

ورحلت نحوك

علّني

في نهدك المجهود

ألقى سر أمسي

وأبوح بالشكوى

الخفيّةْ

٢

بالرمو

يا خيمة

يتجمع العشاق

تحت ظلالها

ما عدت أعجب

كيف أجمع في هواك

العَاشقون

من الصحارى

From her breath

Soft fragrances exude.

In the company of my sweetheart

I journeyed unto you,

In the hope of laying

The secret of my heart

Upon your weary bosom

And to confess my hidden agonies there.

II

Palermo.

A tent you are.

Lovers assemble beneath your shade.

No longer do I wonder

How lovers—whether of desert

والبحار

الآن نهدك

يستباح

بلا حميّه

أم أن عينيك

التي جمعت

فتون الغَانيات

تثير في الفرسان

نخوتهم

فيصارعون الموج

كي يحظوا

بنظرتك الأبيّه

٣

بالرمو

ها نحن جئنا

عاشقين

وعلى رموش

34

Or of sea

Can be of one mind in your love.

Is it owing to your full breast,

Which stands defenceless

Before its violators?

Or do your eyes,

Which gather the charms of all the beauties,

Still inspirit the dauntless knights

To feats of gallantry?

Driving them to combat waves

Just to attain one haughty glance.

III

Palermo.

Here we come,

As ardent lovers.

And on the eyelashes

حَبَيبي

مليون شاردة

وذكرى

وعلى جبيني

مليون خاطرة

شجيّهْ

٤

بالرمو

بالأمس

كنا الفاتحين

ولنا على

قمم الحياة

علامة لا تستباح

ولا تباح

واليوم صرنا

سلعة تُشترى

Of my beloved dwell

A million fleeting images

And recollections.

On my forehead reside

A million thoughts.

IV

Palermo.

In days gone by,

We were the victors

Who made their mark.

A mark borne high

On the crests of life.

A mark inviolate

And impermissible.

Yet this day

We have become

Feeble and bashful,

بأسواق المزاد

الحر

خائرة حيّه

٥

بالرمو

ها نحن قد جئنا

نناجي العشق

في عينيك

ونزور مقبرة

المآذن

والمساجد

في ربى نهديك

خامدة شقية

ونبدد الخجل

القبيح

بألف خاطرة

نديّه

At free auctions

To be sold.

V

Palermo.

Here we come,

Love exchanging secrets

In your eyes.

Hoping to visit a cemetery

Of minarets,

And of mosques.

Of a life, extinguished,

And a misery made manifest

On the mounds of your breasts.

Hoping to allay

A shame most loathsome

With a thousand dewy thoughts.

حينما يورق الصخر

يا جذوة الايحاء

يا فجري الأغر

ان ابعدتنا غفلة القدر

وان توارى

عن خيالنا القمر

ففي سمانا.. يسكن القمر

إن نحن جئنا

نستتر

فالشمس حينا تستتر

كي يستريح الكون

كي يهدا الضجر

لتعود.. نشوى تنتشر

تهب الحياة.. وليدة

When Stones Foliate

O flame of inspiration!

O morning of my glory!

If fate's inadvertence has drawn us apart,

If the moon chose to wane

From the slate of our fancy,

In this sky of ours . . . the moon resides forever.

If at times we hide ourselves,

The sun too hides its face.

For the world must take its rest

And tedium must abate.

It must return . . . intoxicated as ever.

Radiating as ever.

Offering a life . . . born in wealth

بالدفء .. بالصبح العطر

ان ذات يوم هب اعصار كدر

أوجفت الصحراء

أوشح المطر

فنحن في فضانا يولد المطر

وتنسج النجوم ثوبها الفضي

كالدرر

وفي ربانا تعشب الرمال

يورق الصخر

ان تلهميني الشعر

أنغام وتر

إن تجعليني .. أعشق السحر

ان تقبس الأضواء

من عينيك

آلاف الصور

ومن شذاك العذب

يقتات الزهر

And a morning full of fragrance.

If some day or other a dusty storm should blow,

Or the desert is exhausted

Or the rain becomes scarce

In our space the rain itself is ever born.

In our space the stars silvery garment is always woven

Like a string of pearls.

In our hills sand may sprout

And even stones may foliate.

If you inspire me with rhythmical poetry,

Resembling tunes from musical strings

If you make me . . . an ardent lover,

Of the hindmost part of the night

If the lights are stealing a thousand images

From your eyes,

If the flowers are being fed from the

Sweetness of your scent,

فذاك .. يا حبيبتي

لأن في عينك للحب

مقر

ومليون نهر

All this . . . my beloved can only be because

Love finds its home

And a million flowing rivers

In your eyes.

المداد

مليون عام

قبل أن أكون

أو تكوني

كنا مداد الحب

في قصائد الحيتان

والرعاة

وأبجدية السنين

كنا ضياء

قرمزياً

يرافق الرياح

والنجوم

والسحاب

ويختبي في بسمة

The Source

A million years ago,

Before I ever was

Before you ever were

We were the source of love itself

residing in the poems sung by whales

and by shepherds.

A light we were

Crimson in colour.

Companion to the winds,

to the stars and

to the clouds.

Hiding in a smile

that dwelt in eyes.

العيون
كنا رموز الوجد
والسر الذي
أوحى لقيس
عشق ليلى
وأشاع أن العشق
ضرب من جنون
مليون عام
قبل أن أكون
أو تكوني
كنا وشوم العشق
في مساحة الأزمان
والأحلام
والحنين
كنا الندى الوردي

We were symbols

for the ecstasy and

the mystery.

Which unveiled to Qays

the reality of his love

His melancholic love for Laylah.

And revealed to all that

Love is a kind of madness.

A million years ago,

Before I ever was

Before you ever were

We were landmarks

of love itself

over the stretching expanse

of unfolding years.

In dreams, as in nostalgia,

We were the rosy dew

في جفاف هذا
الكوكب الحزين

مليون عام
قبله
وبعده
نظل قصة
وردية
خطت بأحرف
الخلود
والصفاء
فوق هامة
السنين
فصولها تحكي
متى بدأتِ
أو بدأتُ
كيف صرتِ
وكيف صرنا الحب

Over the dryness
of this grieving planet.

A million years ago,
Before the planet's birth
And after it
We shall go on being
an ever-rosy tale.
Inscribed with letters
of purity and immorality
Perched on the crown of
unfolding years.

When did I begin?
When did you begin?
How did I come to be?
How did you come to be?
And how did we both happen to be

في سفينة القرون

مليون عام

سوف نبقى

قصيدة العشاق

والسمارْ

ونغمة

تبدد الشكوى

من الحرمان

والشجون

Love itself in this vessel of centuries?

A million years to come,

We shall remain

that tender poem of lovers

And of friends

nocturnally confabulating.

That melody,

which dispels all lamentations

From denial's bosom

Or from plaintive stirring

which arises in the soul.

نجوى في زورق

(مهداة الى صاحبي في الزورق التائه)

١

في الزورق

بين شوك وزهور	إن في الأرض نباتاً
تأبانا العبور	نحن في الزورق والأمواج
والموج يثور	عاصفات تتحدى الموج
نتغنى في حبور	عبثاً نبدو سكارى

Soliloquy in a Boat

(Dedicated to my friend in his drifting boat)

I

In the Boat

On earth exists a plant which
Possesses both thorn and flower.

We are in a boat
Our passage denied by rising waves.

The storms pose a challenge
The waves rise in their giant billows.

In vain we act like drunkards
Singing as if we were happy.

واجتنب دنيا الغرور	حطم اليأس برفق

٢

اشراق

فقد طال المغيب	أدر الزورق نحو الشط
انه الفجر القريب	انظر النور فهيا
بين حلم ونحيب	قد كفانا ما قضينا
واملأ الأرض لهيب	أفرغ الجو هتافاً
فمدى الخطو رحيب	فرق الاشطان واخط

Gently break the desperation
And spare this world of vanity.

II

Sunrise

Turn the boat towards the shore
We have been absent for too long.

Behold the light and let us move
Dawn is close at hand.

Enough time we have spent
In spells of reverie and bewailing.

Astound the surroundings with fiery outcries
And fill the earth with flames.

Untie these ropes and step forward
For the scope is truly vast.

تحدّي

كما يبدو شديد	وجّه الزورق فالموج
رغم اصرار العنيد	سوف نعلو إن عزمنا
غير صخر لا يحيد	انبذ الكأس فلسنا
كنا، قساة لا نبيد	سوف نبدو غيرما
والأماني في مزيد!	قيمة العيش أمان

III

Challenge

Steer the boat for it does not seem
That the waves are rough.

Victorious we shall be
Despite an unyielding sceptic.

Relinquish the goblet for we are nothing
If not like rock, unwieldy.

We shall remain—contrary to appearance
Truly tough and indestructible.

The value of life is in what we yearn for
And what we yearn for, is on the rise.

٤

حكمة

خالد منذ الأزل!	جوهر الكون صراع
كفاح وخطل!	حكمه ان الحياة
الحلم بأشراق الأمل!!	فلنودع زورق
بين جد وهزل!	فترى الكون مزيجاً
ما فتبدده الشعل	تكتسي الدنيا ظلا

IV

Wisdom

The essence of being is a struggle
Perpetual since all eternity.

It ordains that life is of the nature
Of strife and of absurdity.

Let us say farewell to the boat of our dreams
With a hope most radiant.

This universe will seem like a medley
Of jest and of earnestness.

The world is apparelled in darkness which
Torches of light will soon dispel.

٥

اعتراف

أو هوان فمنون	كلنا يحيا فعزٌّ
فأنا لحني حزين	فاحمل القيثارة عني
واترك الماضي الدفين	وتغنَّ في صفاء
جمعنا من شئون	أنت مني وأنا منك

٦

حقيقة

تغطيها الغيوم	لك دنيا مثل دنياي

V

Confession

We all live life—be it in honour or abasement
Until death is upon us.

Carry the lyre in my stead
For my tune is now sorrowful.

Sing away free of cares
And let the past be buried.

You are from me and I from you
Gathered from many an affair.

VI

Truth

This world of yours—like that of mine
Is cloaked in dark clouds.

في سبيل الحق والايمان   نستحلي الحميم

فلماذا لم تكن مثلي   سعيداً بالهموم ..؟!

الشقاء المر للروح   غذاء ونعيم !!

فاملأ الكأس شقاء   وأشرب النخب حميم

For the sake of truth and of faith
One deems it sweet to taste mortality.

Why are you not like I am
Happy in burdens?

For bitter affliction is solace
To the soul and a felicity.

So fill the chalice to its brim
And drink a toast to death itself.

بَقايا السنين

١

أتوق اليك

كفجر ندي

يعَانق في مقلتيه

بزوغ الضياء

وهمس الشجر

وأهرب مني

اذا ما ضجرت اليك

واجعل من ظل رمشك

مكان لجوئي

ومن مقلتيك

ربيعي النظر

The Remains of the Years

I

I long for you

like a dewy morn

Embracing with its eyes

the break of dawn

And the rustle of trees.

When I fall, I flee

to you from myself.

I make of your eyelashes

My place of refuge,

I make of your eyes

My blooming spring.

٢

شربت من العشق
مليون كأسٍ
وكأسٍ
ولم أرتو
وجربت كل صنوف
الغرام
وما كان قبلك حب
وما من سكر

٣

ركبت سفين السنين
وأبحرت في عين كل محار
وما كنت أعرف
لون النهار

68

I drank from love
A million and one goblets
without quenching my thirst.

I sampled all kinds of love;
What passed before you
And what came after you
Yet illusive drunkenness
was nowhere to be found.

I boarded the ships
of the passing years
I sailed in the heart
of every seashell.
Knowing nothing of the
colour of day;
Knowing nothing of the

ونبض الرياح
ونغْم الوتر
وناجيت كل
البروج
وكل الفصول
وطال على قدميّ
السفر

٤

ظننت بأني
بقايا السفين
وأني ولدتُ وعشتُ
بألف هويةْ
ودون هويةْ
وأني نسيج من الحب
يهوى السفر

rhythm of the wind

Nor of the tunes of musical strings.

I implored all

The constellations of heaven

All the seasons of the year

Until my feet grew weary

from the extent of my travels.

IV

I believed I was

The remains of the years

And that I was born

and that I lived

With a thousand identities;

Yet without one

And that I am like a

Tissue of love

In love with travel;

وملّ السفر

٥

ويوم أتيت
إليّ
على صهوة العشق
وفي ناظريك
يطل القمر
وحلم العمر
نسيت شجوني
وكل سنيني
وأدركت أن حنيني
اليك بفعل
القدر
وأنك مبتدئي
والخبر

Yet tired of it.

V

The day you came to me
upon love's well-appointed seat
And in your eyes
The moon beamed down
with a dream of a lifetime,
All my sorrows and
All my parched years
were just forgotten.

I came to see that
Yearning for you was
the doing of destiny
And that, to me
You are the beginning
And the end.

غربَة

من قال: بأن الغربة

حدث جغرافي

ينأى فيه الجسم عن القريه

وتظل النفس حبيسة

جدران الغرفة

فيحن الجسم الى العودة للنفس

فتكون الغربه

حدثًا ماديًا ساحرًا

Exile

Who can say that exile
Is just an accident of geography?
In it the body has to reside
At a distance from the village.

In it the soul stays confined
Within the walls of space
And so the body longs and
Pines for the soul.

In this view exile becomes
A material event
By which the mind
Is somehow bewitched.

من قال بأن الغربة أُن تبقى

خارج سور القريه

تبحث عن أُفق آخر

تسترسل فيه وجودك

تحسب أُنك تزرع فيه

بذور العوده

نحو وعودك

نحو الفردوس المفقود

البَاهر

تغمس فيه أُظافرك المبتورة

حتى اليأس

تثقب فيه جدار الخوف

من المعلوم

تحرق فيه حنينك للغربه

للتجديف ببحر مجهول الأعماق

مجهول الأبعَاد

بحر ليس له آخر

تبحث فيه عن الضالين

Who can say that exile

Is to remain outside the walls of a certain village?

To search for different horizons

In which to unfold your being.

There to plant the seeds of return

To a paradise lost

To dip your clipped nails

To the very limit of desperation

To pierce the wall of binding fear.

There to burn a longing

You feel for exile

For rowing in a sea

Of a depth unknown.

An endless sea in which to search

For those who are lost

Apart from yourself.

سواك

عن مأوى ليس له جدران

عن ظل ليس به ألوان

ترقب فيه حنين العودة

للأرض الأم

للزمن البكر الطاهر

ترسم فيه طيوف الأحلام

تقفز فيه حدود

النسيان

وحديث الجدة عن عالم ما خلف

البحر

عن قصة فرسان العهد الغابر

In which to look for some refuge

Which has no walls

For some shade which is colourless,

Wherein to watch

Your own longing for return

Return to the motherland,

To the age of innocence

And of purity

Wherein to paint the true colour

Of your dreams.

Jumping over the seeming limits

Of forgetfulness,

Reaching out for tales of the past;

The tales of a grandmother.

About the world beyond the sea.

About the knights

From bygone days.

من قال بأن طيور الهجرة

تعبر درب الغربه

حين تهاجر

أو أن البدوي الباحث

عن مرعى شتوي

أوي صيفي

يستشعر معنى الغربه

حين يسافر

فالغربة احساس بالوحدهـ

في عمق الزحمه

الغربة أن تشعر بالبعد الذاتي

وأنت قريب

أن يصبح طعم المألوف

نشازاً

واللفظ المألوف

غريباً

Who can say

That the birds which take

To flight in migration

Are on the road to some exile?

Or that the Bedouin

Who takes to travel in his search

For winter pastures

Or summer waters

Can thereby taste the meaning of exile?

Exile is to feel you are alone

Even when you are close to someone

It is when the taste of familiar things

Becomes repelling.

And when a word

Once thought familiar

Is strange to the hearing.

الغربه أن ترتد الى الداخل
أن يصبح احساسك بالعودة عاقراً

Exile is rebounding to the very inward

Sensing return

As something sterile.

أميرة العيُون

تقول لي أميرة العيون

يا سيد الحروف من تكون

مغامر تراك في الهوى

أم سائح تريحه الشجون

أم غارق في عشق من ترى

والعشق لوتدري من الجنون

Princess of Eyes

Princess of eyes

O master of letters,

What can you be?

An adventurer of love

Or just a wayfarer

Who finds his response

In sorrowful thoughts?

Or could it be

That you are immersed

In a haunting love

Of some apparitions

Which come and go?

فقلت أني كل هذه

أبحرت في الرمال و"العيون"

وتهت في السراب والنوى

وذقت من أوارها المنون

وحين لم تكوني بينها

أقفلت مرتداً إلى الظنون

For love—if you know it
Is like a spell of madness.

I said to her,
I am all the things you say
For I have sailed
In the vast expanses of never-ending sand
And in springs of water.

I have lost my way in the
Shimmer of mirage
And in separation,
Tasting death in the fury of the furnace.
Not finding you,
I chose to return
And so to fall back on my doubts.

وذات ليل رائع الصفاء

أتيت حلماً باهر الفنون

وحينما أفقت صرت لي

الحب والرجاء والفنون

وسوف أبقى ها هنا غدا

وأحتسي من لحظك الحنون

One wonderful night

Of pure luminosity

You came

Like a dream of enchanting imagery.

And on my awakening

You have come to be

Like love to me,

Like hope

And like all the arts

Fused in a single reality.

In the morrow

I shall be here,

To slowly slip the piercing glances

From your eyes.

تحَـدي

حطمت جدار
الصمت...
كسرت حزام الخوف
وخرجت من الزنزانة
رمزاً...
وخرجت من الزنزانة
طيفاً
يجتاح سكوني
وعبرت الأسلاك الشائكة
الملغومة.. بالاحباط

Challenge

You destroyed
The wall of silence.
You broke free
From the zone of fear.

You came out from
The prison cell,
An Illusion,
A Vision,
Penetrating my silence.

You have crossed barbed wire fences,
Which were mined
With frustration.

وطمرت حواجز حرّاس
التعب المكبوت..
كالصوت.
دخلت على المحراب
ومددت إليّ يديك
ومددت اليك شجوني
وفرشت لقلبي..
من قلبك سجاداً
لأصلي وفي قربك صليت

You have buried the barricades

Once erected, by those

Guarding a suppressed weariness . . .

Like a sound,

You entered the niche.

Your hands reaching

Out to me,

As my sad thoughts

Reached out to you.

From your heart to mine,

You spread out

A prayer mat

So that I could pray.

And I said my prayers

Next to you.

وفي بعدك أدنيت
وفي عمقك أبحرتُ.. وأبحرت
وما زلت على ظهر سفيني
وسأبقى بين الموج وحيد
وسأصرعه..
وسيبقى الحب..
نديمي

In your remoteness,

I drew near.

And in your depth,

I sailed . . . And sailed.

I am still aboard my

Sailing ship,

And there I shall remain

Alone, amidst the waves

Which I shall vanquish.

And love shall remain

My close companion.

قوس قزح

ما بين الصحوة والحلم
وملايين الأنجم
جئت كالنجمة
تختالين اليّ
وبين عيونك
قوس قزح
وأنا أعشق وهج الألوان
بعينيك
وأعشق
قوس قزح
هذه لحظة
ابحاري.. في عالمك المسحور

Rainbow

In between

Dreaming and wakefulness

And a million stars

You came to me.

In your eyes there dwelt

A rainbow.

How I love the brightness

Of colours.

How I love the rainbow!

This is the moment

Of my sailing.

في عالمك

الزاهي

تدنو....

وأنا أرقص

كالمزيور

بليل فرح

هذه لحظة

عتقي

لحظة

عشقي

أسبح ضد التيار

بين سيوف

الرحمة

والاغراق الروحي

كقوس قزح

In your world

Of enchantment,

Of incandescence

She comes,

Whilst I dance like one possessed

In a night of nuptials.

This is the moment

Of my adoration.

Against the tide I now swim

Amidst the swords

Of pure mercy

And of spiritual inebriation

Like a rainbow.

يا طائري

يا طائري أنت مثلي تعشق الغسقا

وتعشق البدر نشوانا ومؤتلقا

الناس تغرق في الأحلام غافلة

ونحن نشقى بحب الصحو والأرقا

O My Bird

O My bird,
Are you like me?
In love with the dusk
And with the full moon
Ecstatic and bright?

The people are drowning
In dreams as they sleep
Whilst we are suffering
The love of being awake
And insomnia.

أعاشق أنت تبغى الوصل تنشده

أم هارب أنت تبغي الظل والشفقا

يا صاحبي للهوى بحر يهيجني

من جرب العشق لا يخشى به غرقا

لو كنت مثلك خفاقاً لطرت لها

أو كنت مثلي ذقت البين والحرقا

Are you a lover

Seeking union with the beloved?

Or a fugitive

Seeking the shade and the evening glow?

O My friend,

Love has a sea

Which inflames those with feeling.

Once in it,

They are not afraid of drowning.

If I were made in your likeness

With flapping wings,

I would have flown to her.

Or if you were made

In my likeness

You would have tasted

The burning of parting

And the remoteness.

درب المحبين أشواك وفوح شذى

أسراره صعبة إلاّ لمن عشقا

The path of lovers is full of thorns

As well as fragrance.

It is full of mysteries

Which form a hindrance

Save for those who are in love.

في الغَار

لا نجم في هذا المساء

الحب صار هو الضياء

والأرض مدت

من أزاهرها

رداء

وعيونك النجلاء تمنحني

النقاء

ومغارة فضية

تحكي أقاصيص الهوى

In the Grotto

Not a star this evening,
For love is now the light.

And the earth extended
from her bed of flowers,
A covering mantle.

Your wide eyes bestow
their purity upon me,
A silvery grotto
relates stories of love.

كانت بقلب النهر

منتجعاً

لأصدافٍ عشقن

بلا ارتواء

لا صوت في هذا المساء

الاّ أنين الوحد

في دفقي

وصوت النهر

يرسمه صدى

وتداعي النجوى وأوتار

تلامسها رموشك

والهواء

It was a resort

for shells of the sea,

All-enamoured

yet never quenching their thirst.

Not a sound this evening

except for moans,

Of poignant stirrings

flowing from me.

And the sound of the river

shaped by an echo,

A succession of whispers

from musical strings

Touched by your eyelashes

and the air.

احساس

ما أجمل أن أحضن

إحساساً أنك في القرب

معي

في البعد معي

نجماً في الصحو

وفي الغيم.

بدون

أفول

ما أجمل أنك صرت

جداول حب

تجرين كما الشلال

بوديان دمي

A Sentiment

How beautiful it is
When I embrace the feeling of you
Close here beside me.

In the separating distance
You are with me
Like a star in a cloudless sky,
Even in the clouds never setting.

How beautiful it is that you should become
Like brooks of love
In the manner of a waterfall
Joyously running through
The valleys of my blood.

في الخصب

وفي الجدب

تأتين

من الأدغال

على فرس

كالاعصار قوي

كالأوتار طري

وأطير رديفاً

نذهب للمعلوم

وللمجهول

In fertile times
In times of drought
How beautiful it is
That you should come
From the thick of the forests
On the back of a horse.

A horse, so powerful
Like a tempest
Yet so pliable
Like musical strings.

And we fly
You and I
Two in a mount
Together we go
To places we know
And to those we don't.

الجنيّة والجرة

سأظل أحلم أنني
جنية في وسط جرة
سأظل أحلم أنني
جنية في كل مرة
وأظل أبحث عن
رؤاك
وعن يديك
عن المعزة
والمسرة

A Fairy and a Jar

I shall go on dreaming
of being a fairy
in the middle of a jar.

I shall go on dreaming
of being a fairy
forever.

And I shall go on
searching;
For a glimpse of you.
For the touch of your hands.
For your affections.
And for a feeling of sheer joy.

سأظل أحلم أنني

لك يا رفيق الحلم

بحراً ثائر الأمواج

أو فردوس جنه

سأظل ماذا؟.

لست أدري أي درب

تبتغيه وأي جره

أنا قطرة من نفح

أحلام ولدن

بلا مسرهْ

فمتى أكون

كما أشاء

كما تشاء..

يا من له حلمي

أسرَّه..

I shall go on dreaming

that to you—O! companion of my dreams

I am a raging ocean or

A garden of Paradise.

I shall go on being....being what?

I know not what path

Or jar you desire.

I am a drop from the breath

of dreams

Born without joy.

When shall I be what I long to be?

What you long me to be?

You, to whom I whisper

The secret of my dreams.

مُسَافران

صحو سمائي أشمس الحب فائتلقي

لا غيم يجرح خد الصبح والغسق

لا شيء يحجب عن عينيك بهجتها

تضيء حين عناق الليل بالشفق

Two Travellers

Love sun-bathed
Shines in my cloudless sky.
Not a blemish may wound
The clear cheek of morning
Or that of falling darkness.
Not a thing may veil
The joyfulness in your eyes.

At that moment,
When the redness of the horizon
Is embraced by the night
Your eyes may glow.
They may gather unto their lashes
And press unto their bosom

تضم في رمشها عيني وتحضنها

فيسمان بلا هم بلا أرق

وينزل الغيث والأجواء صافية

غيث وشمس وأمواج من العبق

فينعمان بأحلام موشحة

يودعان عناء الشهد والحرق

مسافران وما زالا مكانهما

في موكب حافل بالعشق والألق

Those of mine.
Unfettered by sleeplessness
They may smile.

In such pure surroundings
Rain may copiously pour;
Like heavenly aid.
Like a radiant sun.
Like waves of fragrance.
They may enjoy such dreams
As are bedecked with adornments.
Taking leave of all their agony
Of sleepless nights and burning pains.

Herein two travellers
Who never departed
From their place,
May partake in a procession
In which love and splendour abound.

عناق

حيث قال البحر للنهر

هلا

والتقى

عند أقدام "متاتا"

كان يوماً

ليس كالأيام

يمشي الخيلاء

حيث كان البحر والنهر

سواء

كنت لي البحر

أو النهر

أو أنا البحر

Embrace

When sea said to river

"Hello"

As they met at the feet

Of Matata[1]

It was a day like no other

Pridefully strutting.

You were to me

Like the sea

Or like the river.

Or in you

I was one with the sea

---

1. A number of caves at the point where the Gironde river meets the Atlantic, in the South-West of France.

أو النهر

سواء

وعناق سرمدي

دافئ دون ارتواء

وطيور ترقب الليل

يضم الموج

ملهوف الجواء

مستعيرا

بعض ما فيَّ

بعض ما فيك

وحداء النهر

يجتاح الخواء

وأهازيج الهواء

And with river

In an embrace

Everlasting.

A warm embrace

Unappeasable,

Where birds watch the night

Enfolding the waves with

A ravenous heart.

Assuming the likeness

Of my inner being.

Assuming the likeness

Of your inner being.

And the river's travel hymn

Overwhelms the emptiness

And the odes

Of the air.

حيث قال البحر للنهر

هلا

والنجوم الغر قالت

للسماء أنا هنا

حيث تجرين

بأعماقي

قضاء أجملا

وتغنينا

تناجينا

أقاصيص الهواء

حيث قال النهر للبحر

إنني مثلك

في العمق

سواء

صار عهداً

إننا نبقى خليلين

ولن نفترقا

Where sea said to river

"Hello"

Where August stars said to sky

"Here we are".

And where you—my beloved

Flow deep within me

Like a fate

Most becoming.

And we chanted songs

And exchanged soliloquies

About the tales of the air.

Where river said to sea

"I am in your likeness deep within—we are as one."

Thus, to us

It has become a covenant

That we should remain as friends

That we should never separate.

طفُولة عشق

إن رمت أن أبقى

نهراً من حب

فدعي طلفي ييكي

يصرخ

يعبث

كالنهر غداة

الاعصار

ان رمت أن

أبقى صبحاً

يسخر بالعتمة

فدعي طفلي

يركض حرا

Love's Playful Child

If you wish me to remain

Like a river of love,

Then leave the child in me

To clamour

And play

In the manner of a river

On a stormy day.

If you wish me to remain

Like a morning

Which taunts obscurity,

Then leave the child in me

To run as it pleases

Free of cares.

يجمع كل خيوط.. الشمس..

ليصنع منه جدارا

ان شئت أن أبقى

غيمة وسم تمطر همساً

لتفيء الأرض

بأنواع الكمأة

والأزهار

فدعي طفلي

يبني من حبّات الرمل

قصورا

ويشكل من صخر

الصحراء

رقيق..

.. الأوتار..

Then, let it gather

Rays of sunlight

And make for itself

A wall of beams.

If you wish me to remain,

Like a promising cloud

Showering whispers,

Filling the earth with flower blossoms

Then leave the child in me

To build sandcastles

And mould delicate tunes

From the rock of the desert.

كابري

كابري ونجومها

ترتاح في حضن السحاب

وترتدي في عرسها الصيفي

أوشاح الضباب

والبدر يغمز من علٍ

يصطاد نافذة يطل بها

ويخترق الحجاب

والنازحون

من التفوق والضجيج

Capri

Capri and its stars

Which rest embraced

By clusters of clouds.

Capri which wears

In its summer wedding

Flowing stripes of mist.

As the full moon winks

From above

Searching for a breach

From which to look down;

And pierce the veil and those émigrés;

From their achievement.

من التطور والخراب

ومزارب منثورة

تحكي أقاصيص الرحيل

وكل ألحان الغياب

والأكهف الخرساء

تنطق.. تستخير

الباحثين عن الرتابة

والتلاقي.. والاياب

والعائدون

From noise.

From progress.

From ruin.

Those scattered impoundments

Telling stories of departure

Singing tunes of vanishing

And all the dumb cavities.

Speak away

They plead with the seekers;

Of tedium.

Of encounter.

And of return.

The ones coming back

The ones fleeing away

From the grinders.

الهاربون
من المطاحن يركضون
كمن يلاحقهم
قطيع من ذئاب
كأسراب الذباب
وأنا أفتش
عنك مغترباً
تطاردني الأنا
كي تحمليني في رموشك
تبعديني
من هذه الحمى العتيقة
والسغب الدفين
من العذاب

The ones on the run

As if being chased

By a pack of wolves.

Chased like flies!

Whilst I search for you

Like one in a strange land

Pursued by the voice

Of a nagging ego.

So that you may hold me

Between your eyelashes

And take me away;

From this aged fever.

From this hunger.

Inhumed in the deep

From this suffering.

فدعي عيونك

تحتوي ظمئي اليك

كما النسيم الرطب

في صحرا

يغلفها السراب

وتصير عيناك

الرضاب

وكل أُصناف

الشراب

Now let your eyes

Embrace the thirst

I feel for you.

In the manner of a cool breath

Laden with water

which blows in the desert

Covered by mirage.

At such time

Your eyes shall become

the moist honey of lips

And all kinds of drink.

الحُبُّ مُشَاع

١

صرنا نشازاً يا رفيقة
في مفاهيم الرُّعاعْ
هذا زمانٌ
صار فيه الدرهمُ المعتوهُ
مرفوعَ الشراعْ
هذا زمانٌ
صارَ فيه العشقُ
منبوذَ الطباعْ

Free Love for All

I

O my friend—

According to the mob

You and I

Have become the odd ones out.

This time of ours

Belongs to the idiotic Dirham

Its sails raised.

This is a time

In which the ways of love

Are being cast out

As things undesirable.

سكنتْ مَنارتَهُ

الضِّباغْ

وتشردتْ أنغامُهُ

في لُجةٍ يحتلُّها

صوتُ الضَيَاغْ

صارتْ مزاهرهُ

تباعُ وتُستباغْ

A time in which

Love's beacon of light

Is turned into home

For the beasts of carrion.

A time in which

The tunes and melodies

Once celebrating love

Are dispersed into a raging sea.

Wherein the voice

Of sheer depravity

Now rules supreme.

Wherein the tokens

Once graced with love

Are mere commodities to be

Bought and sold.

رُجمَ الهوى في الشعرِ
وامتُهنَتْ حروفُ
النَّثْرِ
وانتحرَ اليَراعْ

٢

زحفَ التتارُ
على النفائسِ من تراثِ
العشقِ
والحسِّ الشجاعِ
وأحْرقوها

144

Even the letters
Written in prose
Reduce all love
To degradation.
Even the poetry
Once honouring love
Stones it to death.
The plume itself
Has committed suicide.

II

The tartars are coming.
They are marching
Into all that is precious
Of the heritage of love.
Burning all!

قطعوا على العشاقِ

خلْوَتَهمْ

وتطاولُوا

واستأصلُوا

من كلِ أقمارِ الهوىَ

وهجَ الشعاعْ

فرضُوا الحصارَ

على البراءةِ

في مناجاةِ الحبيبِ

حبيبَهُ

حتى غدا همْسُ القلوبْ

بدعاً وسُخْريةً

وأسراراً تُذاعْ

سقَط القِناعُ

عن التلبسِ

والتصنّع

والخِداعْ

ها نحنُ نصْمُدُ وحدَنا

They rudely intruded
Into the sanctuary of lovers
And plucked all the lustre
From love's shining moons.
They imposed a blockade
Of the innocence of love
On the secret communion
Of those who are in love.

The whispers of hearts
Become a thing out of place
A pitiful object for ridicule.
A saucy secret to broadcast.
Hence, all the masks
Have fallen off
Never more to be worn.
Even guile and pretence
Went down the same route.

ها نحنُ نعزفُ

نَاينا

في أُذنِ كل الخائفينْ

من التلفظِ

والسماعْ

مدّي إلى قلبي

يديك لِتلمسي

نبضَ الإرادةِ

أن أُحِبْ

وتمرّدي في وجهِ

من زعموا الرُّقيْ

وهمو بدنيا اللهوِ

من سقَطِ المتاعْ

III

We alone stay resolute

In keeping the spirit.

We alone play our flute

For all to hear.

For all who fear to utter a word.

Extend your hands

To touch the heart

And feel the pulse of my will—

My will to love

And my rebellion against the ones

Who are full of pretensions

To be advanced.

Those who revel

In a world of abandon

Like worthless objects

Dropped by life.

هاتي عيونَكِ

ترقُبُ الإصرارَ

في عيْني

تُحصّنُهُ

وتمنحُه الإرادةَ

للتصدّي

والدفاعْ

٤

الدرهُم الموتورُ

ظلّلَ سِحْرُهُ

كلَّ النفوسْ

أخْفَى لها السمَّ

الزُعافْ

وصار هاجِسُهُ

مُطاعْ

والمتْخَمونَ

كما الجِياعْ

Bring your eyes
To stiffen my resolve
And bestow upon me
The will to confront,
The will to defend.

IV

Beware my friend
The guile of the Dirham,
The embittered Dirham
Has cast its shadow.

It hid its poison in every soul.
Its every whim
Is now a rule to be obeyed.
And the ones who are fattened
With the ones who are starved

يتناهشونَ

بَقيّةَ الإحساسِ

في القلب الصفىّ

وفي النُّهَى

يَتَقاسمُونَ فُتاتَهُ

يتقاتلونَ

كما السباغْ

وأنا وأنت شريحةٌ

ورثَتْ

حقوق الطبعِ

في سفْر الهوى

منذُ الرَّضاعْ

Are all mauling one another
For the last bit of sentiment.

The last, left behind
In a heart that is pure
In a mind untainted.
They divide the crumbs
And fight each other
In the manner of beasts.

Yet you and I
Are that one piece
Which inherited
All rights of print
To the book of love.
We have come
By our heritage
Even as babes
Still being suckled.

وسنَحْملُ المصباحَ

للجيلِ الذي

يوماً سيأتي

وسنزرَعُ الحبَّ البريءَ

بَرحْمِ أزمانٍ ستأتي

حتى يصَير الحبُّ

كلُّ الحبِ

في الدنيا مُشاعْ

We shall carry high

The beacon

For a generation

Yet to come.

We shall plant this love

Full of innocence

In the wombs

Of times to come.

Until such time

When love,

All love

Becomes free for all.

لا يُشرى الحبَ

العين المتعبة الخرساء،
يغالبها الإعياء
تقاوم اغفاءات النوم
الأبديةْ.
ونداء اليأس:
تردده الأصداء
يغازل ريح الصحراء الرمليةْ
والليل يُخيّم فوق ركام القرية
ثكلى
ويدق بأيد باردة
غربيَةْ

Love May Not Be Bought

The weary dumb eye battles on

against exhaustion,

It resists the eternal bouts

of creeping slumber.

A call of despair is

Being echoed,

Repeatedly it flirts with a sandstorm

that rages out in the desert.

And the night covers that

which remains

of a village bereaved,

With cold Occidental hands.

وأنين الأرض المنحورة،
فوق جدار الشهوة
تستجدي حشرجة الإجهاض
الأزليةْ
والطفل الضائع
بين براءات الحلم
وتفاهات الأشياء
المرسومة فوق وجوهٍ
خشبيةْ
وعويل الشاعر
يلهث مبحوحاً،
مهزوماً،
يرثي ملحمة الأمس،
ونداءات الفخر
الشعبيةْ
وعواء الريح
يداعب أكواخاً حبلى
بالبؤس،

The moans of a slaughtered land
atop the wall of desire,
Are begging and begging
for the eternal shriek of miscarriage.

A lost child caught between
the innocence of dreams,
And the grim reality of the
things marked on wooden faces.
A poet wails and pants
with emotion,
Defeated, he bemoans
An epic of the past.

The public calls for a boastful glory
and a hauling wind,
Caressing some hovels
Pregnant with misery.

وشجون النقمهْ

والأسماء

العربيهْ

ويد راعشةٌ

تقبض بالغليون المحشوِ

هذاراً

تمتد

لتسرق آثاراً

محمّيهْ

ويد اخرى مثقلة بالقيد

يراودها الحلم

بأن تكتب

إفلاس التاريخ

بأيد شرقيهْ

ونعيق

يستجدي اليأس مصيراً،

ويبشّر أنَ رياح الإنقاذ

رياح غربيّهْ.

The pains of rancour
and the Arabic names,
The trembling hand
clasping a pipe stuffed with talk
of a garrulous nature.
It is extended to steal the well-guarded
sites of ancient glories.

Yet still other hands heavy with chains
Are dreaming to write
about history's bankruptcy
With Oriental hands.

An ugly croaking begs incessantly
to make despair
A fate acknowledged.
It announces gladly that the
winds of salvation
Are Occidental winds.

وعلى منضدة اللعبة

يجتمع الأضداد

جهاراً

كي يقتسموا الكون

مجالات

حيويةْ

وعلى مقربة:

يجلس شيخ

قد درس التاريخ

ويدرك معنى الأضداد،

يردد

أقوالاً منسيهْ:

لا يُهزم شعبٌ

شاء صموداً،

لا يشرى الحبُ

لا تغتال..

الآمال البشرية

At the game's table the opposites meet

to openly divide the world's vital fields.

And still close by an old man sits

One learned in history and steeped

in the knowledge

Of the opposites in question.

He repeats some sayings

Now long forgotten.

No people shall be vanquished

who are willing to resist.

No love may be bought,

No hopes of humanity may be assassinated.

يا شجر الطلح

يا شجر الطلح طفا ضجري

في زمن الجدب وشح المطر

لا فيء بظللك يورفني

ملساء فروعك كالحجر

جرداء غصونك باهتة

توحي باليأس وبالضجر

O Trees of the Acacia

O Trees of Acacia
I am filled with boredom to the point of overflowing,
In this is time of drought
And scarcity of rain.

You are without a shade to welcome or surround,
With stone-smooth branches
Void of leaves
There is nothing to hold on to.

Your denuded boughs
In their faded shabbiness
Can only evoke thoughts
Of tedium and despair.

خرساء شجونك هامدة

بلهاء رموزك كالخدر

Your stirrings of melancholy

In their utter dullness

Make tiresome symbols

That only feel like numbness.

دُولار

دولار

هذا الورق العَاهر

عفواً

هذا الورق الساحر

هذا الزحف القاهر

هذا الإعصار

دولار

هذا الرمز الجبار

ينُّ كان، ريال

أم دينار

Dollar

Dollar!

This desolate piece of paper.

Sorry! I mean;

This fascinating piece of paper.

This irresistible march.

This raging storm.

Dollar!

This all-powerful symbol;

Be it Yen.

Be it Riyal.

Be it Dinar.

من منا .. لم يأسره

بريق الدولار؟

دولار

هذي النعمة

عفواً

هذي النقمة

هذا الجني القادم

عبر بقايا الاصرار

دولار

درب.. ملايين الأسفار

لحن يعزفه

الأضداد سوياً

كالجوقة

عود، مزمار، طبل

Who has never been enthralled

By the glitter of the dollar?

Dollar!

This blessing.

Sorry! I mean;

This blight

This goblin

Coming across the remnants

Of persistence.

Dollar!

This open road of

A million journeys.

This melody played in concert

By foes.

Like a musical band;

One for lute.

One for flute.

قيثار

دولار

هذا السقط.. الآسن

هذا البدل الأخلاقي

هذا المرض العصري

هذا الإحباط الممزوج

بطعم الإعسار

دولار

وتتيه الأفكار

ما بين نداء الروح

الغارق في لجج الزحف الكلي

وما بين الشبق المادي

تضيع الأفكار

وتحكي الأسرار

One for drum.

One for harp.

Dollar!

This raging entity prematurely born.

This moral substitute.

This modern disease.

This frustration mixed

With the taste of hardship and toil.

Dollar!

Thoughts wander off,

Between the call of spirit

Submerged in the endless abysses

Of total invasion.

Of material lust.

Thoughts wander off,

Uncannily revealing the secrets within.

دولار

شيء يمرق كالإعصار

ينفذ كالحب

بلا إنذار

يحرق كل حصون العفة

ما بين يمين

ويسار

دولار

حسب الفهم .. دوار

حسب العمر مزار

لكن

ما أقسَى أن تدرك بعضاً مما يفعله

الدولار

Dollar!

A darting thing.

Like a raging storm

Piercing unannounced

As if it were in love.

Burning every armour

Before seeming virtue;

Be it left.

Be it right.

Dollar!

By the measure of wit . . . it is pure vertigo.

By the measure of age . . . it is a sacred shrine.

Yet what a cruel thing for one to realise

Some of the awesome deeds performed by

The Dollar.